RUINED TO RECOVERY

Help when the affair is discovered

by

Brad and Heidi Mitchell

Printed in the United States of America
ISBN 978-1-7341588-2-3

Published by

Build Your Marriage
BuildYourMarriage.org

As a marriage and family therapist who has seen firsthand the devastating heartbreak of couples going through the trauma of an affair, I find the story of Brad and Heidi's recovery not only compelling but full of practical wisdom and insight for any struggling couple looking for a blueprint to follow as they navigate these uncharted waters. With practical steps on how they were able to rediscover each other as well as recover a vibrant spiritual life, this is a book that I believe God will use as a powerful tool to take any marriage from ruined to recovery.

Robert Barrows. Th.M, (Dallas Theological Seminary) M.MFT (Liberty University)

With humility and vulnerability, Brad and Heidi Mitchell share a brave book...brave in its honesty, brave in its sharing and brave in its desire to offer a healing pathway for other couples who are experiencing shame, ruin, and the end of a marriage because of infidelity. Keep this book in your library. It may be the help someone is desperately seeking.

Valerie Bell
CEO Awana®

Brad and Heidi Mitchell continue to challenge couples with a forthright yet humble approach. As a mental health therapist that engages with many couples who are navigating infidelity issues, this is a must-have resource! I will be using it extensively in my work with couples in need of healing and restoration.

Scott Hundley
Board Certified Christian Counselor
Director of Community Downtown
Columbus, Indiana

For our parents,
John & Luann
and
William & Marilyn,
who consistently lived
a faithful and
Christ-centered marriage

CONTENTS

INTRODUCTION

They were ruined.

It was about 11 p.m. on a weeknight. She was getting ready for bed. She had just pulled back the comforter when her husband said he needed to talk to her. He looked strange, different. He knelt next to his side of the bed — and said the words she never thought she would hear. "I'm so sorry, but I've been unfaithful to you."

The words ricocheted through her mind. Had she heard him correctly? What was he doing on the floor? With whom had he been unfaithful? How could this have happened? How had their marriage gotten to this place? What was wrong with him? Stunned and in shock, she responded, "With whom?" Tears filled her eyes.

The rest of the night was a sleepless blur. Sadness, uncertainty, hurt, anger, and fear-filled her mind. *We've been married more than 25 years — how could he have done this to me?* her restless thoughts demanded to know. *What was he thinking? Did he even love me anymore? What would my future be? Would we be getting divorced and if so, when? Could we repair the damage? What about the kids? What would our families say? What about his job? After all, he was in ministry. What about our finances? And do I have the strength to even survive this betrayal by the man I love?*

Wrestling through the night with these questions, she began to get sick. Really, horribly, gut-wrenchingly sick. Over six days she lost nine pounds. The life she had known and enjoyed was gone. The future seemed bleak and scary, the present nothing but a nightmare. Who could help her walk through it? Where could she go for help? Who could she talk to about this? She felt so alone and afraid.

Years ago, that was my (Heidi's) story. My husband, Brad, and I had recently moved to another state far away from my support system of friends and family. We had lived in that new state for only six weeks when Brad confessed his affair to me late that September evening. Life was about to become very, very difficult. Brad resigned from his job as a pastor of a great church. We lost his salary, our health and dental insurance, and some friends. We lost respect, and we lost the innocence of our marriage. We couldn't afford rent or a mortgage. A semi-retired couple invited us and one of our children to live in two of their bedrooms.

That was all ahead of me, though. All I knew at that moment was that life as I had known it would never be the same. And that somehow, I was going to have to make it through that hour, that day, that week — I had no idea how. I was ruined.

For me (Brad), I had committed adultery. Through a series of unwise choices, I did what I thought I would never do. I built layers of deception in my world and broke my marriage covenant with Heidi. Our relationship went straight into turmoil. My job as a pastor was immediately terminated. Family and friends were devastated. I was ashamed, embarrassed, and broken. I was fearful of the future and uncertain of what would happen in my marriage and family. I was ruined.

We didn't know if we were going to make it. All we could do was process life one moment and one day at a time. Jesus' words rang true in the dailiness of our journey: "Therefore do not be anxious about tomorrow, for tomorrow will be anxious for itself. Sufficient for the day is its own trouble" (Matthew 6:34).

Our story was almost immediately exposed to the public. We were embarrassed to attend our church, so we chose another large church nearby where we could hide in the back row. We didn't feel we belonged in community with other Christians in any Bible study or small group. We felt isolated, sentenced forever to a marginalized marriage in a spiritual wasteland.

Gratefully, God had different plans for us. He does for you as well. In the pages of this book, you will find wisdom and insight that we have gained through our own journey to recovery, and through the help we received ourselves. We aren't professional

counselors. We're fellow travelers on this painful, dark journey
— and travelers who have emerged into the light.

Thankfully, God led us to a godly counselor named Bob who
helped us heal. Over time and with Bob's godly insights, we were
able to repair our marriage. It wasn't easy. The work was hard.
But today we stand together as a testimony to the Lord that with
Him all things are possible — even the restoration of a broken
and damaged marriage. And we want to help others discover
what God can do, too.

Several years into our recovery we started a ministry called
Build Your Marriage. We have a passion to help couples build
Christ-centered marriages. But we're a testimony to the fact it
doesn't always happen without severe bumps along the way. We
are writing this book for others who may have suddenly found
themselves on a path similar to the one we had to walk. We're
writing it, too, for couples who are still recovering from old
wounds.

Your spouse may have been unfaithful to you years ago, and
yet the pain is still with you today. Maybe you've known for
several months that your spouse has been unfaithful and you're
hurting. Perhaps you just found out in the past week that your
marriage vows were shattered. Or maybe your wound is so fresh,
you are in the first few hours after the discovery of an affair. You

may be wondering, as Heidi was, "What do I do? Can somebody please help me? Where do I begin?"

Or you may be the one who, like Brad, was unfaithful to your spouse. You have either confessed or been found out. Now you don't know what to do. Your thinking has been messed up and you don't trust yourself anymore to make the right choices. You are broken, you want to make amends. If possible, you would like to save your marriage.

If you are either of those people, then this book is for you. Or you may be a relative or close friend of someone whose marriage is in trouble. If so, this book will help you guide them on a path toward healing and recovery.

Throughout the book, you will find references to "the offended," the spouse who was betrayed, and "the offender," the spouse who was unfaithful. We have written this book as a "triage manual" to shed light on the first steps to take — and landmines to avoid — when the affair is discovered, and you feel ruined.

The first section is for the offended spouse, when the shock of discovery and emotional trauma leaves you unable to think straight or know what your next steps should be. As you read Heidi's story, you will no doubt resonate with her pain. Sections will leap out at you with direction and counsel you've needed.

Heidi provides thirteen important practices that will stabilize your thinking and direct your road to recovery.

Section two is for the offender. Now that the sin is exposed, a flood of thoughts, emotions, and fears will be pulsing through you. Brad provides thirteen practices to move through in the days ahead. Each requires humility and courage. With God's help you can do the work necessary, and follow your road to recovery.

The final section is for both of you, the couple who chooses to restore their marriage. Having walked this journey ourselves, we have experienced God's hope infused into our relationship. We've seen shattered dreams rebuilt into a mosaic more beautiful than we could've imagined possible. Our hope and desire for you both is that you will experience God's healing at the deepest recesses of your souls. We want you to know his love for you and his hope as you allow Jesus to bring you from ruined to recovery.

PART 1

To the Offended

Morning came and with it the realization that last night's nightmare was no fictitious dream, but my new reality. Feeling very much alone, I tried to gather my thoughts and focus. My husband had had an affair. I didn't want it to be true, but I knew it was. I was devastated. I didn't know where to begin. My future was unknown and unknowable.

Maybe this is where you are today. What should you do? Where do you even start? Here are some steps Brad and I think will be helpful for you.

BE SAFE

The first thing to consider is your safety. Are you safe at home? Is there any chance your spouse will physically harm you? If you have any question about your safety or that of your children, go immediately to a safe place.

Even if you feel safe physically you may be so hurt by your spouse that you want to leave your home. We are not attorneys, but we've been informed that for legal reasons it is always best to consult an attorney before moving out permanently.

Or perhaps your situation is similar to ours, and there's no physical danger in view if you remain in your home. Then stay there. Avoid making rash decisions based on your sudden and changing emotions. You are in shock. You may not even be able to process thoughts coherently. Even though the pain is gut-wrenching, this is a time for self-control and for listening to the wise counsel of others.

BE HELPED

This is probably the most difficult journey you'll travel in your life. You'll need wise counsel as you make decisions and navigate choices. We can't emphasize enough the importance of finding a godly Christian counselor and meeting with them as soon as possible. We were blessed with a wise, godly Christian counselor named Bob. (We still talk to him even after all these years.) I'll never forget my first conversation with Bob. He was very empathetic and empowering. And I needed to feel empowered.

We encourage you especially to stick with a Christian counselor, one who is pro-marriage. There are many good secular counselors, but a Christian counselor has a Biblical view of marriage. Marriage is a covenant between a husband and wife and God, which we trust you agree is true. Therefore, it's essential to meet with a counselor who holds the same worldview. If you don't know of a good Christian counselor, search for "Christian marriage counselors" on the web or call a Christian ministry like *Focus on the Family* or *FamilyLife*. You can also contact larger Bible-believing churches in your area and ask them for the names of solid Christian counselors.

Make sure you do your research, but still if, after your first few appointments, you and your counselor don't connect, then try another counselor. It's essential that you feel comfortable with the beliefs and personality of your counselor because you will be spending a lot of time with them.

At this juncture, you should not even think about whether or not you want to stay married. It's premature. You are thinking too far ahead, and besides, the question takes too much energy. It may be a struggle just to get up, eat, and go to work. You may sleep too much or not enough.

We highly recommend meeting with a Christian counselor as quickly as possible. If your spouse won't go, then go alone. You need it now for *yourself*, not your marriage. A Christian counselor can help you reign in your thoughts and keep you centered on Jesus Christ. This is so important because your emotions will be all over the map, and your thoughts will be, too. A counselor helps you to discern what is true, what is false, and what is unknown. He or she will provide accountability and a safe place to vent. This is what Bob was for me.

BE WELL

Your body has just experienced incredible trauma. Some experts liken it to PTSD, post-traumatic stress disorder. You will probably have physical reactions. You may lose your appetite, vomit, be unable to sleep, sleep too much, experience great anxiety, or be overwhelmed mentally. You may shake, be irritable, sad, angry, or cry. This is all normal. Because of the trauma to your body, though, it is important to eat and stay as healthy as you can. Take vitamins and all your medications. Your physical health matters, so make it a priority to stay well.

Some people in this situation may overeat; others may not eat enough. I tried to eat, but for the first several days I couldn't keep any food down. Keep trying. Eventually, you'll be able to eat again. If several days pass and you are still vomiting, contact your doctor.

Although your sleep schedule may be interrupted, go to bed and try to get several hours of decent sleep each night. You think more clearly and make better choices when you have adequate rest.

Try to maintain a routine. Anything that brings regularity is comforting; it serves as a temporary reprieve from the pain of the revelation. If you can go to work, do it. Continue to exercise. If you're not someone who exercises regularly, then go for walks. A change in environment, whether it is walking or driving in a car, can bring temporary relief from the pain of sitting at home. One of my favorite things was to walk alone on the beach. It helped me process my thoughts while also enjoying the beauty of God's creation. Do something that will be good for you both mentally and physically — because you need to stay well.

Be tactful

The fourth step in your process involves thoughtful communication with others. Whom do I tell and how do I tell them? You'll need to use discernment here. Part of me just wanted to tell everyone what Brad had done. I wanted to be supported and affirmed. But I also knew that Brad and I might decide to stay together, and that what I communicated about him could have the potential for long-term consequences.

Because Brad was a pastor at a large church, there was no way to keep his infidelity a secret from our family – or our congregation. Our situation became public within days, which created another set of issues with our kids.

If you're wondering if you should tell your children or not, we think there are many factors to consider and no situation is exactly alike. So here are a few questions to ask:

- Will your children learn of the infidelity if you don't tell them?

- How old are your children?

- Do they live at home or are they young adults in college or living on their own? Are grandchildren involved? Are your children married?

- What else is occurring within the family? Is another family member ill? Has a grandparent recently passed away? Have you recently moved? Has a pet died? Have either you or your spouse lost a job in the past month or so?

- Are you and your spouse in agreement to tell (or not tell) your kids? Do you and your spouse tell your children together? Or will one spouse reveal the infidelity anyway?

Because our situation was public and our children were older, we decided to inform them. Honestly, this was one of the most difficult things we've ever done. They were heartbroken. You'll want to be prepared, though, for your kids to react in different ways related to their personalities and their physical proximity to the situation.

We strongly suggest that each child be given the opportunity to meet with a counselor to work through the pain they will be experiencing. Don't let the financial cost stop you from making this offer. It is well worth the expense for the long-term emotional and spiritual health of your family. We can't emphasize this enough. When considering whether or not to tell your children, definitely get your counselor's input on the question. Then follow their counsel.

Along with your children, you'll have to determine which of your friends you are going to tell and how you are going to communicate to them. It is very difficult to phone your friends and share such bad news. Our situation was public from the beginning, so I sent out a mass email to our closest friends stating the facts. I refrained from criticizing Brad in the email. You don't want to burn bridges despite your pain. Be tactful.

Here are some questions that may help you think through what to reveal to whom:

- How will the knowledge of your spouse's unfaithfulness affect your family or friends?

- Is it necessary to inform this person? Are they really a close friend or am I seeking sympathy?
- Is there someone in your family, or a good friend, who struggles with bitterness or unforgiveness?
- Is there a person in your circle who already has issues accepting your spouse or just doesn't like them?
- What are the consequences if I don't tell this individual?
- Have I prayed about who I should tell?

Maybe for now you'll decide to hold off on telling certain persons until you are further down your journey of recovery. Again, talk to your counselor about these issues and take his or her advice.

On the other hand, godly friends and family members can be a great resource for spiritual encouragement and support. They were for me. My friends remembered me with gifts, cards, emails, and phone calls. Their acts of kindness reminded me that I was loved and not alone. You need wise, godly friends who can pray for you and with whom you can confide. Tell at least one or two friends who are trusted confidants.

Also, talk to a pastor or ministry leader at your church — though be sure they value marriage, have a strong relationship with the Lord, and will keep confidences.

BE INTENTIONAL

When you are hurting, it is tempting to make quick, rash decisions. You'll be feeling shock, even if you had your suspicions previously. To face the reality that your spouse has actually betrayed you is unbelievably painful. You may feel like packing up your things and moving across the country. Or quitting your job, or throwing your spouse's belongings out in the front yard, or calling the person your spouse had the affair with and screaming at them, or wrecking your spouse's car, or harming yourself or your spouse. Don't do it. Don't sink to the offender's level.

Instead, calm down, try to think as rationally as you can, consider the consequences, and pray for the Lord's peace and wisdom to flow into your mind. Stay focused on the Lord and practice restraint. The best decisions we make are usually those that have been well thought out and prayed about. Seek wise counsel before making decisions of any consequence. Take time to pray and ask for God's wisdom. He will direct your steps (Proverbs 3:6). Then when you do move forward you can do it with confidence and intentionality.

BE SAD

Closely related to the previous step is allowing yourself to grieve. All infidelity involves painful loss. You've lost the innocence of your marriage. You've lost trust in your spouse. You may have actually lost your spouse. You may have lost close friends or in-laws that you loved. Maybe, too, you are losing an income, home, possessions, neighborhood, a church family or school community. You may be losing the dream of a long marriage with your spouse. You feel ruined.

Just today I talked with a woman who told me that her husband of 20 years had decided he doesn't want to stay married anymore. Sobbing, she said, "This is the man I love. We were supposed to grow old together." When a person faces this kind of pain, they can't just recover overnight. It will take time. Your world has been rocked, your dreams shattered.

So don't feel as if there's any reason you shouldn't cry or feel heartbroken. Grief is normal. You may even be furious at your spouse for what they did to you and your family. It's okay to be angry, though the Bible tells us "in your anger do not sin" (Ephesians 4:26). Do not allow your anger to turn into bitterness or revenge. When we allow that to happen, we've crossed over the line into sin.

As you grieve, remind yourself that the pain you're currently experiencing won't last forever. Right now, yes, your grief is raw and all-encompassing. You can't imagine life without pain. It may sound trivial, but it's still true, and worth remembering: You will get better. You can recover.

When I first learned of Brad's infidelity, I couldn't stop thinking about it. I remember one evening several months after his revelation sitting across from him at the table and thinking, "Will there ever be a day that I don't think about this?" It was ever-present; in fact, I was dealing with some new ramification every day. You know what, though? Today I rarely think of it. I can go for days, weeks, and months without even thinking about his betrayal. Now that's the grace of God! As you heal, you can expect to experience the same. There will be brighter days ahead. With God's strength, you will get through this.

Be boundaried

It's important to establish some boundaries with your spouse immediately. One who is unfaithful has shown poor judgment and deceived thinking at the very least. Your spouse did not respect your boundaries or those of your marriage. He or she was being selfish. Their focus was on themselves.

Your spouse may or may not express remorse for their sin. They may desire to stay in your marriage, separate, or pursue the other person. Your spouse may request things of you that wouldn't be appropriate or wise, so it is really advisable for you to set up some boundaries. Some examples would be:

- Don't defend your spouse's choice to be unfaithful.
- Don't allow your spouse to define you. Your identity is in Jesus Christ.
- Don't assume the blame for their sin. Even if you haven't been the perfect husband or the perfect wife, the perfect cook or provider, no one ever deserves to be cheated on. Your spouse made the choice to be unfaithful. You are not responsible for their choice; they are.
- Don't rescue your spouse from the consequences they are experiencing. That's enabling them. Sometimes the only way an unfaithful spouse will repent and grow is by feeling and experiencing the magnitude of their consequences.
- Don't allow your spouse to continue a relationship with the person they had an affair with and also with you. Your spouse must end the relationship with the other person immediately. In other words, your spouse needs to choose: It's you OR the other individual.
- Don't spend time together as a threesome. If your spouse says he or she can't decide between the two of you, then you make the decision for your spouse.

Speak with your counselor about appropriate boundaries and next steps to take.

Initially, at least, don't share with your spouse your deepest thoughts, plans, or desires, or the advice that your counselor is giving you. Because your spouse has been living a selfish and deceptive lifestyle, you'll want to observe their patterns of repentance and healing. Sharing your strategies, plans, changes you hope they make, or your counselor's advice could lead them to simply parrot back what you are seeking, as opposed to truly changing out of repentance. You can let your guard down later, as time goes on and your spouse demonstrates genuine repentance.

BE CAREFUL

This may sound strange, but many couples have sex when they have experienced the trauma of an affair in their marriage. For one or both partners, having sex seems like it will lessen the pain and attract them again to each other. Some couples think of sex as an escape from the painful reality of the present situation.

We believe, however, that God created sex within the context of marriage, and although you still are technically married, that bond has been severely injured. Sex itself has been misused and tainted. It's no longer just the two of you who share that very private and spiritual experience. A third party now "knows" your spouse in the most intimate way and that creates pain.

We suggest you still hold hands and kiss if you desire, but making love should be reserved for a husband and wife who share a committed marriage together. With your marriage vows having been broken, your commitment to each other is probably unstable. Until *both* of you are committed to your marriage, we suggest refraining from lovemaking.

Waiting does several things.

First, waiting begins to rebuild trust. You may need to see that your spouse can exercise self-control in an area where it was lacking.

Second, sex may trigger painful memories for the offender, or it may cause you to imagine all sorts of ugly scenarios. (Such thoughts and memories are additional reasons it's essential to meet with a counselor not only through the revelation phase but also throughout the recovery period.)

Third, when you wait to make love it may help you feel valuable and respected again. Your spouse is demonstrating that your relationship isn't based on sex. You want to be reassured of your worth. Waiting to make love until you're ready shows concern for your well-being.

Fourth, having sex without a sense of trust and commitment can wreak emotional havoc on the betrayed spouse. One minute he or she will be desiring physical closeness and then the next moment he or she will regret having been so intimate.

The apostle Paul wrote to the church in Corinth about married couples abstaining from sex. He said, "Do not deprive one another, except perhaps by agreement for a limited time, that you may devote yourselves to prayer; but then come together again, so that Satan may not tempt you because of your lack of self-control" (1 Corinthians 7:5). You are entering into a season of prayer and discernment about staying in your marriage. Your abstaining, for a time, will help you hear more clearly from God.

Lastly, because your spouse had sex with another person, there is the risk that they could have a sexually transmitted disease. Before you resume making love with your spouse, both of you should be tested. This is humiliating, but it's a necessary step in your recovery and if possible, the restoration of your marriage.

BE GODLY

At this time in your life make sure you prioritize spiritual growth. Although it is desirable to grow spiritually as a couple, what we are referring to here is developing your spiritual life as an *individual,* separate from your spouse. Make sure you are attending church regularly. (Ideally, you would attend together, though you still would want to be concentrating on your own spiritual growth.) Listen to worship music or read a good book. Perhaps you'll want to join a Bible study. You needn't feel like you have to share with everyone what is happening in your marriage, but having other Christians in your life will encourage and strengthen your faith.

If you are not yet a follower of Jesus Christ, this is certainly a good time to make a fresh start and commit your life to Him. Jesus paid the price for your sins — and those of your spouse — on the cross with his life and shed blood. He offers forgiveness of sins, the indwelling presence of his Holy Spirit in you, and eternal life when you invite him into your life as your Leader and Forgiver. If you have never made this personal decision for yourself, we urge you to say a simple prayer to him in your own words, acknowledging that Jesus paid the price for your sins on the cross with his shed blood and life. Thank him for his sacrifice for all of your sins. Ask him to come into your life as your Savior from sin. Tell him you want him at the center of your life; that you want to follow his plans for your life.

Again, take a moment right now and just think about your life. Contemplate what it would mean to have Jesus at the center. If you have made a commitment to Jesus as you are reading this book, the next step is to begin to take action to grow spiritually.

When Brad's affair was revealed, I decided I would make that an intentional effort. Brad and I attended church together. I went to the women's Bible study that I had previously led, although someone else took over leadership. I knew that my source of strength must be in the Lord. Even though I had no idea what the future held, I knew that I could trust God with my future.

What or who is your source of strength right now? Is it your spouse? Your career? Your income? Your parents? Friends? True direction and comfort can only come from God, so he needs to be the One we depend on not only in a crisis but every day.

I knew that for me to become more Christlike I had to grow in the area of my thought life. I had been in the habit of reading my Bible and praying daily, but it soon became evident that I needed to retrain my mind as well.

I decided to do two things in that effort. First, I watched a sermon online each day. I knew of some solid pastors and churches, so I went to their websites to find sermons. As I watched these sermons and thought about them, filling my mind with God's principles, I began to grow spiritually through retraining my mind.

Second, recognizing that my thoughts were often sinful toward Brad, I decided to concentrate on a different Bible verse every day. I bought a book that had a Bible verse for each day of the year. Every time I had a negative thought about Brad or marriage, I would repeat that day's scripture verse over and over. Although I could not see everything it was doing for me at the time, by practicing self-control over my thoughts I was retraining my mind. The Bible gives us a blueprint for our thought life: "Finally, brothers, whatever is true, whatever is honorable, whatever is just, whatever is pure, whatever is lovely, whatever is commendable, if there is any excellence, if there is anything worthy of praise, think about these things" (Philippians 4:8).

We are to evaluate what we choose to think about. Resist the urge to let negative or false thoughts just camp out in your head. Did you know you have control over your thoughts and what thoughts you allow to linger in your mind? You do! Ask yourself these questions to help analyze your thoughts:

- Is this thought true?
- Is this thought consistent with God's Word, the Bible?
- Does this thought contradict any of God's promises or commands?
- Does this thought devalue another human being?
- Am I wanting revenge?
- Am I rationalizing sin - my own or someone else's?

If you are struggling in the area of your thoughts, here are some Bible verses you may find helpful to memorize:

2 Corinthians 10:5 (NIV) "...we take captive every thought to make it obedient to Christ."

1 Peter 5:7 (NIV) "Cast all your anxiety on him because he cares for you."

Philippians 4:6-7 (NLT) "Don't worry about anything; instead, pray about everything. Tell God what you need, and thank him for all he has done. Then you will experience God's peace, which exceeds anything we can understand. His peace will guard your hearts and minds as you live in Christ Jesus."

Nahum 1:7 (NLT) "The Lord is good, a strong refuge when trouble comes. He is close to those who trust him."

Romans 12:17 (NLT) "Never pay back evil with more evil. Do things in such a way that everyone can see you are honorable."

Psalm 4:8 "In peace I will both lie down and sleep; for you alone, O Lord, make me dwell in safety."

2 Corinthians 5:17 (NLT) "This means that anyone who belongs to Christ has become a new person. The old life is gone, a new life has begun!"

2 Chronicles 20:12b (NIV) "We do not know what to do, but our eyes are on you."

Proverbs 3:5-6 (NLT): "Trust in the Lord with all your heart; do not depend on your own understanding. Seek his will in all you do, and he will show you which path to take."

BE DISCERNING

You are in a season that requires discernment. Discernment means to make good judgments from what you observe and perceive. At its root, discernment means to judge, to separate, to tell what is good from bad, true and counterfeit.

There were two questions I had to wrestle with that brought clarity to my decision on whether to divorce Brad or to stay and work on our marriage:

1. Is Brad repentant?

Saying you're sorry isn't the same as repentance. A person can express sorrow for what they did, or feel bad they were caught and still not intend to change their ways.

In our case, Brad apologized for his affair immediately. But I needed time to see if his actions revealed true repentance. 2 Corinthians 7:10 says, "For godly grief produces a repentance that leads to salvation without regret...." Repentance looks at the pain inflicted on God and others. A repentant person grieves over what they have done. They say, "I never want to do that again and so I am going to change with God's help." It's reversing course and turning from the path of sin. The offender recognizes they have sinned against not only their spouse, but more importantly, God. I saw this in Brad.

So how do you tell if your spouse is repentant? The best gauge is their willingness to engage in the healing of your marriage. They won't be perfect, but you can tell if they are sensitive to you. Is your spouse patient with your healing process? Observe them. Do they defer to you? Do they show empathy? Are they genuinely grieved by their sin and its effect on others? Have they relapsed? Are they defensive?

The second question I had to discern had to do with my own heart and relationship with God:

2. Am I released from our marriage?

Biblically, I knew that I had grounds to divorce Brad. But was that what God wanted me to do? Should I leave Brad, or, having discerned genuine repentance, should I stay and fight for our marriage?

I knew that if I decided to stay in our marriage, I couldn't renege on that decision months or years later. I wasn't holding a wildcard I could throw out on the marriage game table 20 or 30 years later. I would be choosing to re-establish the covenant of our marriage. Over time I was able to see his repentance. The storm that was raging in my soul began to quell, and I discerned God wanted me to stay. And I wanted that too.

There's no checklist for you to determine if you're released or not. The best test is your spouse's evidence of repentance. People from all perspectives will offer advice. Your decision, however, is ultimately between you and God. Pray a lot.

BE FORGIVING

Whether or not you and your spouse rebuild your marriage, you'll still need to come to the place in your recovery where you forgive your spouse. This is even more difficult because the person who should be supporting you through these most trying days of your life is also the one who's caused you the greatest pain in your life. But if you don't forgive your spouse, the enemy will plant a seed of bitterness within you. Your spiritual life will be severely harmed by it. The Bible warns of the consequences of an unforgiving heart. We can forgive with Christ's authority for our benefit, so that the enemy won't outsmart us (2 Corinthians 2:10-11 NLT). Luke 6:37 also speaks to the importance of forgiveness when it says, "...forgive and you will be forgiven."

Frequently people get confused about what forgiveness is. Forgiveness is *not* a feeling. In fact, you may not *want* to forgive your spouse. You feel like your spouse has ruined your life. You feel justified holding on to your bitter resentment, considering what they have done to you and your family.

We have *all* sinned, however. Every one of us. No one is immune to sin. Since God forgives our sins when we confess them, we need also to forgive those who've wronged us, even our spouse. We have to grant them forgiveness even if they never ask us for it. Jesus suffered on the cross for the forgiveness of your sins. He bled and died for you. He took the punishment of death so that you could have eternal life.

So follow the example of Jesus and forgive your spouse. Forgive them even if they're not sorry. Forgive them even if they don't apologize. Forgive them even if they choose to leave your marriage. Forgive them if they desert your family. Forgive them even if they are mean and unkind. Forgive them if they lie. Forgive them if they are unrepentant.

"Really?!" you ask. Yes, really; because Christ himself set the example.

You may be thinking, "Okay, so I know I have to forgive and I don't feel like it. How do I begin to forgive them?"

First, acknowledge that forgiveness is *not* a feeling. It is an act of your will. Our feelings don't always equal truth. You need to determine that you are going to forgive your spouse with God's help, and you'll do this out of obedience to God. Count on it: As you practice forgiveness, the feelings of forgiveness will follow in your life.

Second, and even more importantly, if you forgive you will have a clear conscience before God. You won't be consumed with bitterness towards your spouse. Experiencing the freedom available only through forgiveness will allow you to move forward.

This will be an epic battle. It means that your desire for revenge or "to get even" will no longer be the focus of your mind. It means recognizing that God is the one who is responsible for the consequences your spouse will suffer, not you. So give to God your desire to get even, and trust him with the results.

We like to say the phrase, "mind, mouth, motion." What we think about, we talk about, and what we talk about, we do. We begin by controlling our thoughts. Our mouth then reveals what we're thinking and finally, our actions will demonstrate what we have allowed our minds to dwell on. It's mind, mouth, motion. There's a powerful verse, Matthew 12:34b (NLT) that says, "For whatever is in your heart determines what you say."

Third, recognize that forgiveness doesn't mean we're supposed to forget what happened in our marriage. The phrase "forgive and forget" isn't accurate because the greater your pain, the more difficult it is to forget. You will always remember the pain of your spouse's infidelity. I do. But as you heal and forgive that pain will lessen.

You may think you need to run to your spouse and tell them you have forgiven them. Don't go too quickly with that. This is between you and God at this point. If you are struggling with forgiveness, talk to God about it. Tell Him you are having a difficult time with it. Ask God to help you forgive. Perhaps you'd like to write out what you are forgiving your spouse for and then talk to God about it in prayer. Ask God to help your thoughts, words, and actions demonstrate forgiveness. Remember mind, mouth, motions.

Finally, don't listen to the enemy's lies. Satan will cast doubt on the sincerity of your forgiveness. He wants you to question whether you've actually forgiven your spouse, or if you even should. Scripture is clear, though — forgiveness is mandatory in the life of a believer, whether or not your marriage recovers. It's the beginning of your healing, so do it.

BE DIRECTIONAL

At the time of revelation, life is overwhelming. I felt crushed by the weight of the decisions I had to make, while also wondering if I should stay with Brad. I met with Bob, our counselor, and he prayed with me and began to calm my troubled mind.

One of the first questions he asked me was, "What decisions do you need to make today?" I didn't need to decide *today* whether Brad and I would stay married. That decision could wait. We had time. But I did have a speaking engagement coming up in about a week. That was a decision I needed to make quickly. Bob and I discussed it and concluded it would be best for me to cancel it.

Bob walked through similar decisions with me by asking, "What do you need to do today?" Or "What decisions do you have to make in the next week?" I felt empowered, making decisions with Bob's help. Things were starting to fall into place. There was even some semblance of order beginning to reappear, despite all the chaos swirling around me. Although I was unaware of this principle at the time, Bob was helping me to do the "next right thing." He was providing direction to me.

Many individuals in crisis have asked us, "What do I do next?" And we always tell them to *do the next right thing*, right there in the moment. It's become a motto for our marriage.

When a person does the next right thing, they start to move in a good direction. Over time, an individual can cover a lot of ground, doing it one small step at a time.

I used to run track. Every runner who has won a race did so by taking a first step. You don't win a race with just one step — but then again, you do. Without the first step, you'll never be victorious. We need to do "the next right thing" throughout today. Then tomorrow we need to do the next right thing, and again for the day after that.

By breaking decisions down to specific choices, and evaluating those options by what is right *based on the knowledge we have at the moment,* we tend to make the best decisions. If we fall down or get sidetracked, we should get back up as soon as possible and resume making good decisions. We should keep going in the right direction; we should do the next right thing.

BE HOPEFUL

You may feel alone. It may seem like nobody understands your pain. God still has not abandoned you, though. In Jeremiah 29:11 (NLT) God says, "For I know the plans I have for you...they are plans for good and not for disaster, to give you a future and a hope." Your world has been rocked, but your life is not over. Better days filled with blessings will come.

Have you ever been in a blizzard? I'm from the north and I've been in a lot of them. In a blizzard, you can't see very far ahead. Once I couldn't even see to the front of the car! It's hard to tell where you are or if you're even going forward. You don't know where the road ends and the prairie begins. It's cold. The view is gray and monotonous.

But then the wind and the snow stop, the clouds disappear, and the sun shines again. Perspective returns; you can see where you are, and you know what direction you need to go. You can resume making progress.

When your spouse's infidelity is first revealed, it's like being in a blizzard. Thoughts swirl around you and it's hard to see where you are or where you are trying to go. If you'll take the steps we've just talked about, though, the storm will subside. Perspective will return. You'll start to have clearer vision again, so you can advance in the right direction.

God has a plan for you, a future filled with hope, personalized just for you. Part of his purpose for this season in your life is to grow you in learning utter dependence on God. You can be sure that as you rely on him, he will direct you. He will show you your future a step at a time as he walks the journey with you. He will never abandon you no matter how lonely you feel. He will give you wisdom if you ask him for it. Your job is to remain hopeful, to discover his plan, and to take the right next steps toward healing.

PART 2

To the Offender

Pain. Chaos! Your secret has been revealed. Your spouse's emotions are raging; yours are confused, tied up in knots. You don't know what to do next. Is there anything you can say, anything you can do, to make things better? Is this it for your marriage? What about your children? Your extended family and friends?

I've been there. I have some idea what you're going through.

I know that no two situations are the same, yet the overarching pain and trauma around the discovery of an affair are universal. Over the past several years I've communicated with exposed spouses from around the world, men and women who have reached out wanting to know if there was hope. They've needed guidance on their next step, hopefully to restore their marriage.

And so do you.

My journey toward recovery began as I reached out to a counselor in our community that I knew. Even before I told Heidi, I contacted Bob to help me walk through the process. He was straightforward: Tell the truth. Don't beat around the bush.

He gave me one piece of advice that thankfully I wasn't going to need. He said, "You have no idea how she is going to respond, so I would recommend that you have a suitcase packed in the trunk of your car in case you have to leave."

I was scared to death. I had been dreading this conversation for a long time, yet I knew it had to happen. I didn't want to live a lie any longer. And now it was impossible to keep it a secret.

It was late in the evening when I told her. I could feel her heartbreak, shock, and devastation. She asked a few clarifying questions and cried softly. I think the shock of what she heard and our daughter being asleep in the next room mitigated any late-night outburst. We slept on separate sides of the same bed. I didn't need my suitcase.

Within 48 hours I had told our children, both sets of parents, and the leadership and staff of the church I had been serving. Before the week was over, I had lost my job. Ninety percent of our income was gone. I had confessed my unfaithfulness during our church services to the congregation I loved. Losing your job is pretty standard for people in ministry. God won't be mocked, and an unholy person who has betrayed the covenant of marriage should not continue to do ministry in that situation.

But that wasn't all. A few weeks later we were homeless as well as jobless. We couldn't afford a place to live, so a semi-retired couple in our church graciously offered us and our youngest daughter their upstairs. It had two bedrooms and a bathroom. We shared our meals with them. That became our residence for the next 10 months.

The first weeks and months were raw. I was surprised how little energy I had for almost anything else. People reached out with emails of encouragement, and I felt bad that I didn't have what it took to respond. I was able at least to find a job selling ads for a television station. I could engage with the very basics of life and processing with Heidi, but not much else.

I had been a leader with vision and direction; now I felt like I was swimming in peanut butter. Everything took major effort now. Everything.

That was years ago, though. Since then, together we've climbed out of the hole I created. It's finally time for us to share some of the life lessons we've learned through it, lessons that may help you, too. Our hope is that this will give you some traction and direction. Obviously, we can't promise that your marriage will be restored. But we can assure you that you can walk this journey; you can regain your integrity, your confidence. You'll find you can begin again to make the right choices in your life.

These lessons will give you a path to follow, and, just possibly, lay a firm groundwork for your marriage to be restored.

BE HOPEFUL

First and most important: Don't give up hope! Yes, you'll be going through very dark days. Expect it. There will be pain. Difficult conversations. Unsettling discoveries about your own character. Interactions with family members and friends, in which you will have to simply listen and own the truth of what you did, and its effect on them.

There's been a huge boulder dropped in your marriage. You could drop an actual boulder in the water, and the waves at the point of impact would be huge, but the further from the point of impact, the smoother the water becomes. For these next few weeks, things will be choppy and unpredictable. You will experience highs and lows. Count on it. Still, you have to go through this season with the hope that things will be better. You need the reminder and confidence that you are not alone.

And it's true: You're not alone. Psalm 23:4 promises, "Even though I walk through the valley of the shadow of death, I will fear no evil, for you are with me; your rod and your staff, they comfort me." Your personal world feels like a prolonged death right now, but you must remember: God *is* with you! He has not deserted you, he's walking with you. Every time you feel despair and darkness closing in around you, make the simple declaration, "I am not alone. God is with me." And then choose to live in that truth.

Read Psalm 51 as well. This was written by King David of Israel about nine months after his adultery with Bathsheba and his directives to have her husband killed in battle. She bore David's child, and David's affair was exposed after the birth. Interestingly, there is no record of remorse prior to David being confronted and the affair revealed. This passage of scripture meant a lot to me in the initial months after the revelation of my affair. It's a prayer of confession, a request of cleansing, and a spirit of contrition.

I want to highlight verse 17, which says, "The sacrifices of God are a broken spirit; a broken and contrite heart, O God, you will not despise."

Your natural inclination will be to think that God has cast you off and written you out of his plans. You may believe you are ruined. That couldn't be further from the truth! Your brokenness and repentance are honoring to him. The sadness you have over your sin is appropriate in the light of a holy God.

He draws *near* to the broken in spirit. He is drawing near to you! And he loves you very much.

Remember, Jesus Christ paid the full price for your adultery on the cross. His word gives strong assurance that your sin is forgiven and that you are cleansed when you confess your sin before God. The Bible promises us, "If we confess our sins, he is faithful and just to forgive us our sins and to cleanse us from all unrighteousness" (1 John 1:9). You may not feel forgivable, but the truth of scripture overrides any feelings you may have. It was your feelings that got you into trouble to begin with, so choose instead to place your confidence in what is true through the pages of the Bible.

In addition, you won't be able to see or know all that God is doing in your spouse's heart. More than ever, they are going to be more reserved, withdrawn, and careful. They need to be. But that doesn't mean that God isn't working in their life as well. Part of your hope is in knowing that even in the unseen things God is active.

Through the season of your adultery, you tried to control your environment, especially the information that your spouse received and the lies you were covering up. Now you are in a new season of knowing that you are not in control. You will have greater hope and peace as you continually place yourself and your situation in God's hands, and trust him for whatever it is he wants to do in your spouse.

But your progress is going to be all self-effort if you don't have a personal relationship with Jesus. He wants to heal and empower you from the inside out, and only he can do it. This is foundational. It's how you can have hope, experience God's forgiveness, receive forgiveness from those you have hurt, and forgive yourself.

So if you have never invited Jesus into your life as your Leader and Forgiver, now is the time to do so! Say a simple prayer to him in your own words, acknowledging that he paid the price for your sins on the cross with his shed blood. Thank him for his sacrifice for all of your sins — including your adultery. Ask Jesus to come into your life as your Savior from sin. Tell him you want to live with him at the center of your life; that you want to follow his plans for your life.

When you invite Christ into your life, he will immediately forgive your sins, come into your life, and never leave you. No matter how dark the days may get you can know that you are never alone. Jesus will be with you and guide you.

There will still be moments so hard you'll want to give up. You won't want to work on your marriage anymore. The discouragement, the difficult conversations, the embarrassment will seem so insurmountable that you can't imagine making it another day. Winston Churchill, the former Prime Minister of the United Kingdom who faced numerous successes and failures, said, "Success is not final, failure is not fatal, it is the courage to continue that counts." Your journey toward recovery will take courage!

Things *will* get better, though. Hang in there. Remember the promise the apostle Paul wrote to the church in Philippi when he was imprisoned in Rome: "I can do all things through him who strengthens me" (Philippians 4:13).

And so can you!

BE DONE

You must sever your relationship with the other person, the one with whom you sinned. *Completely.* Yes, he or she may be reeling with consequences of what the two of you did. You may feel a sense of "moral" obligation to them because of your role in the affair. Their path may be more severe than yours, or less so. But they can no longer be someone with whom you have *any* contact whatsoever. Returning to the relationship that caused so much pain and devastation would be unwise and destructive to your recovery in every way possible.

That relationship may have felt so right, but you must recognize how dangerous that feeling can be. Your mind could still be flooded with memories, conversations, and connection.

Things that were broken in your marriage were fulfilled in your affair, or at least they felt as if they were. You gave your heart to the other person; now you are embarrassed, torn, ashamed, and fearful of the repercussions in your marriage and life.

For all these reasons, the "safe" place could feel as if it were to be back with the other person. With your spouse feeling sad, angry, aloof, or all three of these, you might want to be with the other party even more, so you can find solace from the onslaught of consequences facing you. To go back to that person would be to risk re-entering a sinful relationship, but for even worse reasons than before, and with the certainty of much greater damage. Now, therefore, more than ever, you need to be done and walk away from your affair physically, emotionally, and mentally.

Your path of healing and recovery will require a single-minded focus on your relationship with God, your spouse, and your family. The Bible perfectly describes having a foot in both worlds when James wrote that a double-minded person is unstable in all their ways (James 1:8). You need stability.

So delete your secret accounts: Facebook, Twitter, Snapchat, email, or any other means of communication with them. Block their phone number. Immediately dismantle any opportunity for contact between the two of you.

Undoubtedly, they will come to mind from time to time. When they do, seize that thought and replace it immediately with thoughts of positive qualities of your spouse. Make a conscious choice not to think of the other person. This re-training of your mind will build new habits of thought toward your mate.

This will require courage, strength of will, and determination, especially at first. Over time, however, the frequency and intensity of your desires for the other person will diminish, while your passion for your spouse increases. It may be too early to know if your spouse will be staying in the marriage. Nevertheless, your personal recovery and growth require a single-minded focus on your marriage.

Additionally, every time you feel the desire to reach out to see how the other individual is doing, offer comfort, or receive solace, choose instead to say a simple prayer entrusting them to God. You may say something like, "God, you are big enough to take care of them. I trust that. I choose to focus on you and my marriage."

You may need to solicit the prayer of a trusted friend to support you against your desire to reconnect. Make a simple call saying, "I am struggling right now. My mind keeps dwelling on the other person and wanting to check in with them, so I'm calling you. Would you please pray with me that I will stay strong and be done?" Bring the struggle into the light, receive the prayer of another, and it will be an invaluable source of strength for you as you move through the process of recovery.

BE TRUTHFUL

Your first inclination will probably be to share *most* of the truth, but not *all* of the truth. Why? Three reasons.

First, you have been living a life of deception, and it's hard to switch gears and immediately be fully truthful. Secrecy must be broken, though, and it must be broken *now*. Pride keeps secrets. Humility and brokenness lives in transparency.

Second, you see the pain your confession has created, and you don't want to increase it more than necessary. Still, the only path from betrayal to healing is honesty. For there to be hope, there must be truth.

Third, you want to cushion the consequences you'll experience from your choices as much as possible. You may think that by not sharing all of the truth, things won't go as badly for you.

But it is precisely because you have been deceptive that you must push toward full transparency. You have to tell all the truth.

You may also be tempted to tell the truth in doses. The thought is that if you tell a little bit now, a little bit later, and stretch it out over a few weeks that it will be easier for your spouse to manage. But telling the truth in doses prolongs the healing and creates greater distrust. You put your spouse in a position of uncertainty and instability. He or she will wonder when the next devastating fact will be revealed. Questions tumble around in their mind: "What *else* have they not told me? How can I really trust them when they aren't being *totally* truthful?"

I will give one caveat. Not all spouses want to hear every detail of your infidelity. Some just want a 45,000-foot overview of what took place. Their imaginations will run wild if they know too much. In our situation, Heidi wanted to know all the truth right upfront. Ask your spouse how much detail they want. Initially, they may not want much. But later, if they ask, be sure you provide it. It may be wise to have a counselor present when you share details.

BE TEACHABLE

Your brokenness will be evident through your teachability. There were things broken in you *and* in your marriage that set the stage for your unfaithfulness. The pain and trauma you both are experiencing is too great to walk through alone. You need a solid, godly counselor who is going to fight for your marriage.

You may balk at the expense of counseling. "Maybe," you may think, "if we get some good books, sign up for some blogs, and watch some YouTube videos we'll soon be good to go and back to normal." Frankly, that's the residue of the same deceptive thinking and pride that got you into this situation. Counseling is simply a natural and necessary consequence of the choices you've made.

The insights of a trained person are invaluable in helping you see what you need to work on next. Good counselors are skilled in facilitating difficult conversations, guiding you to develop new habits, and helping you construct boundaries for your marriage and other relationships. Counseling will create a safe space for your spouse to process their path toward recovery as well. In addition, the accountability created through the counseling experience will be invaluable for you.

Be ready for months of counseling. Stay humble and receptive to the counselor's insights. Even if your spouse chooses not to stay in the marriage, you will need the direction of a gifted counselor to help you repair the broken places in your inner world that made you open to adultery. Often the individual who commits adultery is seeking someone who will complete them, someone who fills the vacuum of their soul. Drs. Les and Leslie Parrott say, "If you try to find intimacy with another person before achieving a sense of wholeness on your own, all your relationships become an attempt to complete yourself." [1]

By contrast, in a healthy marriage each spouse is whole individually and together they create a union as they follow God's purpose for their lives. Each spouse recognizes that they don't complete each other; instead, they complement each other.

Through your teachability with the counselor, you will become more healthy and whole. You will regain your ability to connect with your spouse more intimately. So work hard on the homework and let God mold and re-shape you.

BE TRUSTWORTHY

Building and maintaining trust must become a practice for you for the rest of your life. I've known spouses who wanted to be trusted within weeks or months of the revelation. They've told the truth, ended the wrong relationship(s), and engaged in counseling, so they want a little "credit" to their account where their spouse will trust them again.

Frankly, that drive to shorten the timeline comes from underestimating the severity of the betrayal. Your spouse's desire to keep tabs on you is a result of the fear and pain they have experienced. It's a consequence they now carry. Your

---

[1] https://www.lesandleslie.com/devotions/the-single-sentence

consequence is to be trustworthy and humble enough to be checked up on at any time.

One of the best practices you can incorporate immediately is proactive trustworthiness. Tell your spouse where you are going and who you are going to see. Let them know when you plan to return. Call or text to let them know if you are running late. Provide access to your phone so they can track you. Give your spouse the passwords *to everything*.

At one point several months into our counseling, Heidi asked our counselor, "Will I ever be able to fully trust Brad again?" He answered, "Not 100 percent." That is a new reality and consequence I've had to accept as a result of my choices.

My proactive efforts to be trustworthy have given Heidi increased peace and confidence. The trust factor has risen meteorically over the years, but it took time, too. I'm afraid our counselor was right: It will never be entirely at 100 percent again, but it's strong enough for us to have a healthy and happy marriage. You can get there, too.

BE GRACIOUS

Psychologists have likened the impact of betrayal in marriage to PTSD-inducing trauma. Don't minimize what you've just revealed to your spouse. He or she is in shock. Disbelief. Anger.

Shame. Grief. It would be impossible for you to know or grasp all that is cascading upon them.

Your spouse's feelings are going to be unpredictable and at times unexplainable, even to themselves. Almost anything can trigger their emotions to cascade, their thoughts to run out of control. So prepare yourself for a long healing process of recovery. This isn't something they will just "get over" right away. Betrayal in a marriage is not the kind of thing someone can just "forgive, forget, and move on."

Think of it this way: The offender cannot tell the betrayed when they should be healed. Or in the legal world, the criminal cannot tell the victim when they should be okay. Each person is unique; each one heals at their own pace. Your spouse is going to need your full support, engagement, and patience in their process toward recovery.

Sometimes your spouse's reactions to you may feel like whiplash. They will desire you, then in a matter of minutes seem repulsed by you. There were times that Heidi wanted me to hold her close or be intimate with her. But then hours later she would have her walls up and not desire any intimacy with me whatsoever.

This confused me. As I processed her reactions with Bob, our counselor, he explained that it is common for a betrayed spouse to desire intimacy and closeness, but once they experience it, they feel that they have become too open and vulnerable, exposed. They recoil to protect themselves.

He assured me that over time it would happen less often. He was right. This is why it is important to stay gracious with your spouse. I never would have figured this out on my own, by the way.

Being gracious meant that I had to view Heidi's healing and process as part of God's discipline and reshaping of my own character. Every conversation we had, every appointment with the counselor, every trigger that set her off or made her cry, was an engagement God was allowing not only for her healing but for mine as well.

In part, this meant that when Heidi wanted to go over the details of what I had done, I had to be totally honest and forthcoming with her. I had no desire to go over it all again. But she did. I can't count the number of times that I retold what took place, in painful detail.

Over time I learned that this was important for her so she could crosscheck my story. Was I contradicting myself? Was I leaving anything out? She needed this, to restore her trust in me. It helped me, too, by reminding me all over again how much I had hurt her, and how far I had gone down my path of deception. These reminders reinforced my resolve to stay pure and faithful from then on, no matter what.

BE REPENTANT

Be repentant. Turn away from your sin. This might seem self-evident, but it's incredibly nuanced in how it is lived out. Repentance isn't feeling sorry that you got caught. Nor is it feeling bad about all the *consequences* swirling around your choices. Sadness and regret don't equate to repentance. They're important, but they're not the same. Repentance at its core means a firm resolve not to go in the direction you had been going. It is a decision to do a 180-degree change.

The spirit of repentance must drive you to engage in humility and grace with your spouse in the days and weeks to come. Your spouse may try to hurt you to the same degree they have been hurt. They may lash out at you in ways that will make you recoil, and possibly even long for the arms of another. They may try to hurt you so that you'll feel the devastation you have brought into their life. Their response is not right, but it certainly is natural.

1 Peter 2:21-23 was a great guide for me through this time. Peter writes, "For to this you have been called, because Christ also suffered for you, leaving you an example, so that you might follow in his steps. He committed no sin, neither was deceit found in his mouth. When he was reviled, he did not revile in return; when he suffered, he did not threaten, but continued entrusting himself to him who judges justly."

Following Jesus' example helped me when engaging with Heidi in painful interactions. I chose not to lash back at her or become defensive. Instead, I would breathe a prayer saying, "God, I'm not going to fight back. She's hurt. I'm entrusting this to you." God's Spirit brought his peace to me and prevented the conversation from escalating.

You may think your spouse's perspective is wrong, or their accusations are unfair. It might seem to you that you're giving them the upper hand by choosing not to defend yourself. Keep in mind, though, it was your pride that drew you into your affair. God is using every encounter with your spouse to reshape you into the Christ-follower you are called to be.

If your spouse has wrong information, factual inaccuracies that are important to what took place in your affair, then you should gently make that known and provide the truth. Being accurate isn't the same thing as getting defensive. One is striving for truth, the other for self-vindication and protection.

Remember, too, that sin is not the same thing as shame. Sheila Walsh insightfully points out, "Guilt says you've done something wrong. Shame says you are something wrong."[2] What you have done doesn't define you. God defines you.

---

[2] Walsh, Sheila. "What if I feel shame?" SheilaWalsh.com 2020

You may want to memorize Romans 8:1. It's a powerful reminder of how God views you. It reads, "There is therefore now no condemnation for those who are in Christ Jesus." 1 John 1:9 is a declaration of what happens when we confess our sins before God. John writes, "If we confess our sins, he is faithful and just to forgive us our sins and to cleanse us from all unrighteousness."

These two verses will remind you that from God's perspective you are cleansed and forgiven. There is no more condemnation from God upon you. Jesus took your condemnation and sin upon himself when he suffered and died on the cross on your behalf. From here on, while there are still consequences to be faced, you can walk in the confidence of knowing that your sins are forgiven. And if God no longer condemns you, you shouldn't condemn yourself either.

BE RESPONSIBLE

It will be natural for you and your spouse to talk about what went wrong in your marriage to lead to your sin. As you do, be very careful not to assign blame to them.

Yes, you made your choices within the context of a marriage where something was broken. Yet it is not your place to make your spouse responsible for your wrong choices. Assigning blame is an effort to deflect responsibility. Your role is to assume full ownership of your decisions, without pointing fingers at your spouse.

Over time, with help from a wise and insightful counselor, there will be opportunities for you to share things that influenced your choices. Trust the counselor to determine when to address those issues with your spouse. If the counselor chooses not to bring it up, or if your spouse decides not to accept it, go back to the overarching principle in 1 Peter 2:21-23. Trust any change that you want to see happen in your spouse and marriage to God. You are not responsible to change or fix your spouse. You are responsible for you.

BE MOLDABLE

As you stay engaged with God and with the process, he will shape you into the man or woman that he desires you to be. There's a powerful picture of God's relationship with the nation of Israel in the book of Jeremiah. It has great parallels to what he wants to do in your life as well.

"So I went down to the potter's house, and there he was working at his wheel. And the vessel he was making of clay was spoiled in the potter's hand, and he reworked it into another vessel, as it seemed good to the potter to do.... O house of Israel, can I not do with you as this potter has done? declares the Lord.

Behold, like the clay in the potter's hand, so are you in my hand, O house of Israel" (Jeremiah 18:3-4, 6).

God will do an incredible thing in your life, beyond what you can imagine. He will reshape your character, redefine your purpose, and bring joy to your life again. He may renew your marriage as well. That's in keeping with his nature and character. Your responsibility is to stay faithful to your spouse, focused on God, and engaged in every aspect of your recovery.

It's natural to want to avoid consequences and pain. It may be that it was pain in your life that drove you into someone else's arms. Healing and moldability mean you must lean into the painful places, that you press into the sharp points of consequences. It's not for the purpose of beating yourself up, though, or for needless hurt. You engage to receive everything God has for you in the moment so that you don't miss the development that he wants to do in you.

BE DISCIPLINED

Your mind may long to replay physical, romantic, or conversational interactions with the other person. You must discipline your thinking not to do that. Make a definite choice right now to reject every whiff of a thought about the other person. How? By saying out loud or in your mind, "I choose not to think about that. I am going to focus on my spouse and pray."

Then say a simple prayer like, "God, I am choosing to submit my thoughts to you. I want to honor you and love my spouse *only*. I reject the wrong thinking in the name of Jesus!"

Mental toughness will guard your marriage. The more you exercise the discipline of the mind, the greater will be the victory and brighter your future.

When we met with our counselor, shortly after my revealing my unfaithfulness, he advised us not to make love until Heidi had decided she was going to remain in the marriage. As he put it, making love is for two individuals in a committed marriage, a covenant relationship. He urged us to hold off on sex until she was certain she was going to stay. We should feel free to have physical intimacy with one another, he said, but we couldn't have intercourse until that decision was made.

In hindsight, this was incredibly wise. Making love too soon would have increased Heidi's feeling of vulnerability, and caused her to pull back even further. But there was an additional benefit as well. Unless it's a purely emotional affair, adultery generally involves a sexual relationship with someone else. My ability to abstain gave Heidi ongoing reassurance that I could exercise self-control and discipline.

Your spouse will need to see discipline in other areas of your life as well. Are you prone to overeating? Practice discipline in what you bring into your body, and your self-control will be a reassurance to your spouse. The same is true with exercise or spending habits. Demonstrate to your spouse that you have the discipline that can lead to change.

Your spiritual life will be an especially important area of discipline. You may feel distant from God. You may feel spiritually numb. Yet this is an area you will need to face squarely, so that you may bring the Holy Spirit's healing to your soul, and reshape your mind to think rightly and with purity.

Perhaps you would start with a book of the Bible that you already enjoy reading. Spend a little time in it every day, followed by prayer. If you aren't sure where to start, you may find the gospel of John or the book of Acts helpful.

Even if your spouse chooses not to stay married, growing in discipline and self-control will help you become stable and trustworthy as a person. Your own self-confidence will grow as a result. Every choice you make to increase discipline in your life will be significant in setting new patterns for how you think and act.

BE IN PURSUIT

You have poured hours of time and attention into somebody outside your marriage. Your job now is to give that same effort (and more!) to the pursuit of your spouse's heart.

It may not be easy. You may not feel like it. Your relationship with your spouse is raw and relationally bloody. All you really feel at the moment is pain, brokenness, and probably rejection, too.

Yet this isn't the time for you to pull away. As I said earlier, you may feel like you're walking on thin ice. You may not know when you will say or do something that will trigger an unpleasant response. Pursuing your spouse is hard. It takes courage. You must press through that; you must show your love, no matter what.

Know that your spouse may now be feeling like they weren't enough for you:

- They weren't good looking enough.
- They weren't young enough.
- They weren't rich enough.
- They weren't strong enough.
- They weren't kind enough.
- They weren't sexual enough.

You get the idea.

Your spouse may carry a great deal of insecurity for a long time to come. The deficit in your relationship is huge, but it is not insurmountable. Your task is to see each day as a new opportunity to reinforce that your spouse matters to you and that you desire only them.

One hopeful place to start is by discerning your spouse's "love language." We strongly recommend Gary Chapman's classic book, *The 5 Love Languages: The Secret to Love That Lasts.* He describes how each of us has a way that we like to show love and receive love: quality time, words of affirmation, physical touch, gifts, and/or service. Learn what your spouse appreciates most. Be proactive in expressing love the way they most like to receive it.

Not every initiative will work. Don't be discouraged. Just be persistent and persevere in pursuing your spouse.

BE A PARENT

Your children will all react differently should they find out about your adultery. Give them the freedom to respond honestly and authentically to you. Just as your relationship has been damaged with your spouse, the same is true with your children.

Your natural inclination may be to shrink back from them. You may feel that you have lost your position of influence or even ruined your relationship with them. Indeed, you probably have lost the footing you once had, at least for a time. They may not want to talk to you or even look at you. They may rally around your spouse. After all, your spouse is the victim. And so are they.

But you *are* still their parent. Continue to remain open to their conversations with you. Show them your love. Be consistent. Let them see your repentance and brokenness as well.

If there are issues of discipline, don't hold back, thinking that you lost your moral authority, your voice as a parent. Don't let them pick up on that and use it to get away with bad behavior. There is still right and wrong. As a parent, you still have the role, responsibility, and authority to train your children in the way they should go. Continue to act in a way that reflects grace and discipline within your home.

In the long run, your family will take their cue on how to treat you from your spouse. When they see your spouse responding (over time) in a healed, loving, and forgiving relationship, it will give them the freedom to re-approach you as well. That can't be rushed. Remember, your primary focus is to be on your spouse, and your children will be watching that relationship.

BE ACCOUNTABLE

It is important that you bring into your life a couple of trusted people outside your marriage, and even outside of counseling, with whom you can talk about your unfaithfulness. Choose persons who are godly, who will love you, pray for you, and who care for your marriage.

The accountability these individuals bring into your life has to be the kind that will tell you what you may not want to hear. They have to be willing to call you out on bad thinking, poor choices, and bad behavior. They need to be persons of integrity who care about you and your spouse deeply.

Furthermore, your spouse should know who they are, because you may be having intensive conversations or communication with them over the next few weeks. Consider asking your spouse to help you think of a couple of people who could fill this role. This will give your spouse a level of security and hope, as they will know the quality of individuals with whom you are aligning your life.

Even today, many years past my affair, I have accountability in my life. I think of it as a wall of protection around my heart and around our marriage. I don't want any breach in that wall, so I am ruthlessly honest with my accountability partner.

And again, be hopeful. During the difficult days when I wasn't sure if we were going to make it or if I was going to be able to endure the process, I would reach out to my counselor and he would say three simple words that aren't that transformative but they were enough for me to make it to the next day and then the next. He would simply say, "Hang in there. It's going to get better."

It did. And it will get better for you as well.

PART 3

To the Couple

It was a cool day in early March. We were at our church in Ohio to witness the wedding of our friends, Ron and Lori. Brad had officiated at a lot of weddings. This memorable and celebratory wedding, though, was unlike any we had ever attended. Why? Ron and Lori had divorced several months earlier and now were remarrying each other! Brad had the privilege of officiating as this couple re-established their covenant of marriage. It was a moving ceremony.

Ron and Lori ultimately survived the pain of unfaithfulness and the revelation that followed. They felt ruined. They walked a dark and uncertain path. Their situation looked hopeless. They made the decision to divorce.

It didn't help. After their divorce, things really hit rock bottom. They cried out to God and he intervened. Repentance happened. Prayers were answered. Forgiveness was granted. And ultimately a marriage was restored. Ron and Lori's kids have mom and dad living together again under the same roof. They are growing in their love for God and each other. They are active in our church and are in the couples small group we lead.

Ron and Lori are a "Cinderella story." Not all marriages, though, can recover from the pain of revelation and betrayal. What has to happen for a marriage to be restored and healed? What steps can you take to rebuild your marriage? How can you as a couple recover? How can you go from ruined to recovery?

BELIEVE YOU CAN HAVE A STRONGER, MORE FULFILLING MARRIAGE

It's hard to imagine your marriage will survive when it's been rocked to the core and you're hurting like you never have before. That's the nature of pain. When we hurt it's all-consuming. Think about when you're sick. You don't care about work, how messy your home is, what you're going to eat, or seeing friends or family. You're focused on your sickness. You wonder when you're going to feel well again. That's all that matters in the moment. And it's the same principle with your marriage.

As time passes you re-engage with life. You start to discover the strengths and weaknesses in your marriage. You work through hurts, insecurities, and the pain of unfaithfulness. You learn how to protect your marriage from betrayal in the future. As your marriage becomes healthier, you grow as a couple. It becomes easier to imagine a fulfilling future together. You see that you can recover — together.

Your marriage has been through the fire and fire refines you. It improves you. It purifies you. Your marriage can be stronger and more authentic as a result of your commitment to heal. The fact that you've survived unfaithfulness and resolved to rebuild your marriage is huge. You've made some important decisions to get to this point:

- You've communicated to each other that you want to stay together.

- You've chosen not to take your marriage — or your spouse — for granted.

- You are learning about each other in ways other couples don't.

- You've discovered where your marriage is weak and are addressing those issues.

- You've been developing a deeper understanding of each other and how the two of you think and interact.

- You are applying new ways to handle conflict and communication.

- You've chosen to grow in intimacy with your spouse and God.

- You can now focus on building a new foundation for your marriage with Jesus Christ at the center.

As you implement these changes in your marriage, you become increasingly hope-filled. You see that you can recover. Though you may be married to the same person, your marriage can be different. Totally redefined. A better marriage. A stronger marriage. A more fulfilling marriage. A Christ-centered marriage. This is the best marriage for you.

CONSIDER THE RAMIFICATIONS OF DIVORCE

"I rebuild my marriage by thinking about divorce?" Absolutely! Considering the consequences can be a powerful deterrent from poor choices. Divorce isn't an easy "escape route." It's fraught with dangerous implications. Take time and think about what could happen. It can protect you from repeating past mistakes.

The Bible is clear that God hates divorce (Malachi 2:16 NIV). He knows the impact of divorce not only on you and your covenant but also on your family. And divorce is more complicated when children are involved. According to the Pew

Research Center, children raised in a single-parent home experience more poverty than those growing up in a home with a married couple.[3]

Beyond financial implications, consider these questions:

- How will divorce impact your children, relationally, and educationally?
- Would you share custody, or would your kids live with one parent most of the time?
- What toll would this take on your children?
- Would they have to move to another house, state, or school district?
- How would this affect their plans for college?
- Could they continue at their current school?
- Would they feel like they have to defend mom or dad, or side with one parent over the other?
- Would their involvement with sports, church, and friends change?

Even if you don't have children, a divorce still costs a lot of money. You will most likely lose any connection you have with your spouse and their family. This severing of family

---

[3] G. Livingston, "About One-Third of U.S. Children are Living with an Unmarried Parent," *PewResearch.org*, April 27, 2018.

relationships and mutual friendships is typically one of the most gut-wrenching aspects of divorce.

How will your divorce impact your family spiritually? Will your kids see divorce as an acceptable alternative when they encounter problems in their own marriage? What example would you be setting for your children to follow? Has God released you from your marriage? Do you have Biblical reasons to divorce, or are you just unhappy with your spouse? Have you tried to rebuild your marriage? Have you done all you can to live at peace one with another (Romans 12:18)?

Is your spouse repentant? Does your spouse want to stay married? Has your spouse forgiven you? Do you want to leave a legacy of divorce for your children and grandchildren?

Thinking through the outcomes of divorce can drive powerful conversations, strengthening your resolve to rebuild. You'll have a check in your spirit each time you feel like getting a divorce. There will be a fire in your gut to do the work to restore and rebuild your marriage with Jesus at the center.

DETERMINE YOUR CIRCLES OF TRUST

We know couples who chose not to speak to anyone about the affair. Their children never found out. Their friends and family never heard about it. For some, that may be the best choice for healing.

You may still each want to confide in a few others, however. Maybe you have already when the affair was revealed. If not, how do you decide who to tell? This is important; it helps establish the environment for healing. Who needs to know? Who can you both trust? Who among your friends struggles with bitterness? Who might try to divide the two of you? And who among them is wise?

Here are a few suggestions as you assemble your circle of trust:

1. Start with a small circle. If your initial inclination is to tell as many people as possible — perhaps to gather support and encouragement, or to feel validated — don't do it. Remember your goal is to build unity and trust. Over the next few days or weeks, you may expand your circle. But it's more prudent to start slowly, carefully, and together. You can always add individuals, but once you've given them information you can never take it away from them.

2. Decide together whom you will tell and stick to it. Sharing this decision helps you start to restore trust in each other.

    As much as possible, predetermine the people who must be informed. Older children, parents, siblings, and a handful of close friends may be in that circle. This is for you to determine and agree on together.

3. Agree together on what you are and are not going to say. Then stick with that plan. You'll create trust and solidarity for your marriage, and in your healing. You don't need to script it out word for word, but you should talk about the key phrases and components that you will share. Some questions to consider are:

- Are you going to call it adultery or an affair?
- Are you going to tell how long it had been going on?
- Will you let people know if the offender was discovered or came forward on their own?
- What specific details do you plan to share with others?
- Are you going to tell people what your next steps are in healing?
- Will you give insights into your personal thoughts and feelings?

We strongly suggest that you refrain from giving any specifics about the other party involved. They have their own journey to walk through. It's not your business to talk about the other person, and it's not others' business to ask, either. If people ask, simply tell them politely, but firmly, that your focus is on the two of you. If they choose to pray for the other individual they can do it without having to know details.

4. Determine which spouse will communicate to whom. We believed it was best for Brad to do the communicating with our family members and children. He needed to own what he did. They needed to hear his voice when he told them. Heidi was present for most of those conversations. This allowed them to either hear her voice or see her face so they could gauge their own reactions and emotions. It was a statement of marital unity even in the midst of brokenness.

It's best if each of you communicates to your close friends independently. You need your own circle of support. (Again, you may have already done this when the affair was revealed.)

5. Discuss how you will communicate. Your only option may be the phone, for example with family members who live out of state and need to know rather quickly. You won't have the time, energy, or perhaps resources to travel and tell them personally. For those who live nearby, face-to-face is better. For people who are on the periphery of your relationship, you may write a

letter. Be careful sending electronic messages, though, whether by email or text. They can take on a life of their own, out of your control, being forwarded to other individuals or groups. It can cause additional, unnecessary pain to you and your family.

6. Finally, breathe a prayer to God before you open your mouth. Invite him to guide you. Whether you and your spouse pray out loud together is your choice. You can also pray silently. Have a prayerful spirit that invites God to speak through you. Ask him to open the ears and hearts of the people who are hearing your story.

What about those you don't inform? Your tears or heaviness of heart may tell them something is wrong. You don't have to volunteer anything. If they ask, you can give them a vague answer like, "I'm just going through a difficult personal time that I really can't talk about. But I sure do appreciate your prayers and encouragement."

DEVELOP NEW HABITS AND SKILLS

Marriage betrayal always highlights areas of weakness. Perhaps you and your spouse don't communicate well. Maybe you "stuff" your thoughts and feelings, while the other explodes in anger. You may take each other for granted. Or you esteem kindness so much, you don't want to offend your spouse by telling the truth.

Wherever you struggle as an individual, a seasoned counselor will bring it to light. To discover your strengths and weaknesses is one of your first steps toward change. Why do you react a certain way? What do you tell yourself? What motivates you? What happened in your past that causes pain and insecurity?

As you learn about yourself, you'll find areas where you need to grow as a couple. Use this new understanding and insight to build your marriage. If you continue to think and react as you did in the past, nothing will improve. Your marriage may seem better for a while, but eventually, the problems resurface and you'll both be frustrated.

So concentrate instead on how you can change. Don't focus on what your spouse needs to do differently. We can't change other people, only ourselves. What can *you* do differently to become a better wife or husband?

You might start having devotions. Or praying together. You could join a Bible study, or launch an exercise program. You could learn how to handle anger or hurt effectively, to speak honestly when you don't agree, or say no when appropriate. You could encourage your spouse more.

Pay attention to your tone of voice and body language as you talk with your spouse. Are you fully engaged or distracted? Are you looking at your spouse? Are your arms folded and crossed? Are you scowling? Show interest in your spouse with your body language and facial expressions.

These are actions you might take but consider your thoughts as well. Are you thinking the best of your spouse? What do you allow yourself to dwell on? Do you tell yourself that you're the only person that matters? Do you feel like you're a loser? Do you believe your spouse is lazy and prideful? Do you feel like you deserve to be treated a certain way?

We reemphasize this because it is absolutely critical to monitor your thoughts. Your marriage won't heal unless you change your thinking. Make sure your thoughts align with scripture and what God says about who you are, who others are, and who He is.

As you implement these skills and practices, you'll want to be sure to develop new patterns with your spouse. Learn how to be proactive and anticipate areas of potential conflict. Discuss how you'll handle stressful situations before you emotionally react to them.

ZIP THE LIP

Early in our counseling, we talked about the other woman by name. It became a trigger. When we mentioned her name we experienced a set-back in our recovery. We couldn't understand why.

As we processed this with our counselor, he made the simple suggestion that we should not bring up her name in any conversations. He said that simply using her name continued to re-insert her into our relationship. We followed his advice, and it proved wise. Tension and triggers dissipated.

So choose to refer to the other person with pronouns like "he" or "she," or talk about "that other person." We found this helped keep the focus on our relationship without bringing the other person into our healing process.

PROTECT EACH OTHER

People love giving advice, whether they know what they're talking about or not. They'll voice a variety of opinions on how you should proceed. You want wise counsel, but ultimately whose advice you heed is determined by you.

Unfortunately, well-intended people may try to divide you. They will tell you that you've tried long enough and it's time to give up. They will point out the flaws in your spouse and their efforts. They may attempt to set you up with someone who they think is a good match for you. Don't listen to their advice.

Additionally, your story, though unique, can create triggers in others who have experienced similar pain in their own lives.

Be aware of the dynamics churning around you as people try to speak into your healing process. Their perspective could be colored by their past.

Extended family may try to take sides as well. They feel the pain of their blood relative and want to support the person they love. Some may even feel embittered toward your spouse. This is natural. You have to have each other's back and protect one another even from family. Open and honest communication is the groundwork for all you do. Don't be offended when others offer advice and you disagree. Encourage each other to think the best of those around you.

Other people will eventually take their cue about your relationship from you — and especially from the attitude of the offended. We have often seen this dynamic at work between the offender and their in-laws. As the offended shows acceptance and forgiveness towards their spouse, other family members usually follow the attitude of the offended. If you forgive, speak well, and think the best of each other, eventually most people will follow your lead and make the same choices toward the two of you.

FACE CONSEQUENCES TOGETHER
Together you will face consequences of one spouse's sinful choices. Count on it. It's unfortunate that the repercussions of

sin affect the offended. But sin's impact often has collateral damage. You are the ones hurting. Your children, friends, colleagues, people at church, and others will also experience degrees of pain, sadness, or hardship.

In our situation, Brad lost his job immediately. He had two weeks of severance pay, then no salary. Heidi had only a part-time job, 15 hours per week. We lost 90 percent of our income overnight. Pressure mounted quickly. Within days literally thousands of people knew about Brad's affair. This created a spotlight on our family and a scramble to communicate to our circle of friends so they could hear from us and not from others. Our lives felt ruined. And the waves of impact kept crushing in on us.

The current and previous churches that Brad served were particularly devastated by his sin. This side of heaven, we have no idea what detrimental impact this had on peoples' spiritual journeys. That's a consequence we live with that cannot be rectified, except by God's miraculous work in a person's life.

With Brad losing his job, we couldn't afford a mortgage or even rent for an apartment. We didn't know where we could live. It was — as you can guess — really awful. Providentially, a semi-retired couple invited us to live upstairs in their home. For the next 10 months we stayed with them. We cooked together with them. We ate every dinner together. We cleaned together.

Eventually, Brad found a sales job, but it still wasn't enough to cover all of our expenses. Meanwhile, we were going to counseling (sometimes twice a week), taking long walks, trying to process what was taking place.

We became very isolated from the relationships we knew and loved. It was lonely. It was hard — really, really hard. We felt ruined.

You have your own set of consequences to face as a couple. It's incredibly painful, especially for the offended. He or she will feel like they don't deserve the pain. Each consequence, when it comes, serves as another trigger and reminder of the pain your marriage is experiencing.

Here are a few suggestions for how to address your consequences:

1. View each consequence as pragmatically as possible. Do your best to take your raw emotions out of it. Take each one in a matter-of-fact attitude, and it will help you think clearly, without reactiveness.

2. Don't use the consequence to blame or shift responsibility. The two of you are on the same team. It is natural to want to turn each new consequence into a chance to inflict more pain on your spouse. It's natural to blame-shift. Guard your heart and your

relationship from doing so. Otherwise, you'll extend the timeline of your recovery.

3. Lean into each consequence as an expression of God's discipline. He is shaping your character and marriage. God allows consequences. Each one is an opportunity to experience the weight of what took place and submit yourself to his wisdom, his provision, and his healing. You have a choice. You can either embrace the consequence or become bitter and angry about it. We urge you to embrace the consequence, no matter how painful, and grow through it.

4. See how God uses each consequence for his glory. Pain is an opportunity not only to grow, but to expand your faith and trust. Look for ways you can acknowledge God as you walk through the consequence. Take time together to pray about each consequence. Ask God for wisdom. Ask God how you can glorify him through it. This one practice alone brings his wisdom to bear as he unifies your souls.

EXPECT GOD'S BLESSINGS

You've chosen to stay together. That's good! But it doesn't obligate God to make everything easy. Intuitively you know difficult days and challenges lie ahead.

When you fight for your marriage and rebuild your relationship, you honor God. You keep the covenant you established when you stood at the altar and declared your mutual commitment to one another. You honor God's presence in your life and the centrality of Jesus Christ in who you are. You are a living testimony to the restorative power of God in broken relationships. And you move from ruined to recovery.

If either of you is unsure about your relationship with Jesus, we want to reiterate what we wrote in each of your "sections" of this book. Thank him for what he did for you on the cross by paying the price for your sins. Invite him into your life as your Leader and Forgiver. Make the determination — together — to base your marriage on following Jesus.

When Jesus taught the story about the prodigal son in Luke 15, he described a young man who essentially wished his father was already dead and wanted his inheritance immediately. The son went off on his own. He rejected the relationship he had with his father and his family. He squandered everything in a sinful lifestyle.

When the son returned home, broken, humble, and repentant, the father welcomed him back with a huge party and a restored relationship. This is how God views his relationship with you. He is thrilled by your choice to stay committed to one another. He wants to celebrate and bless you for your choices! God wants to pour his favor upon you.

So watch for signs of God's blessings to you. Start a "blessing book" and write down each time you identify favor from him. Let this book become a holy testimony to God's activity in your life. When things get hard or you are discouraged, read this book. Your entries will remind you of the many ways God has worked in your marriage. This will give you hope, confidence, and faith for the days to come!

CONTINUE IN COUNSELING

You may meet with more than one counselor before you find someone you both agree on. Once you find a counselor who is godly and supportive of your marriage, stick with them. We have watched couples move from counselor to counselor once things became difficult or personal. This is just avoiding what it takes for you to grow and heal. Counselors often challenge couples on their thought processes or decisions. It's hard work, going through counseling. It takes commitment to persevere. Hang in there.

It's not uncommon for a couple to begin counseling and within a handful of sessions feel like they have gotten on a good track — so good, they feel like they can handle the rest of their recovery on their own, without help from a counselor. (Not surprisingly, we have observed that often it is the offender who is most eager to step away from counseling.) This is almost certainly premature and unwise.

Dr. Stephen Judah writes, "...give yourselves at least a year to get back to level ground. Research reveals that couples who have stayed involved in a counseling process for nine to eleven months experience the best outcomes."[4] This is your opportunity to grow as an individual and as a couple. You don't want to miss the steps to recovery God has for you through a gifted and well-trained therapist.

Realize, though, the counseling process can be intense. In addition, the conversations about the affair when you're at home can be so pervasive that one or both of you will simply feel emotional fatigue. We recommend that periodically you agree to a 24-hour or full-weekend moratorium on talking about the affair. Give yourself the freedom to take a much-needed break. Allow the dust to settle and bring freshness into your conversations a day or two later.

BE ROMANTIC

---

[4] Stephen Judah, *Staying Together When An Affair Pulls You Apart* (Downers Grove, InterVarsity Press, 2006), p. 164.

What drew you to each other when you were dating? What activities did you enjoy? Where did you like hanging out? Did you hold hands in public? Did you take long walks? Did you cuddle? Did you have long talks as you gazed into each other's eyes? Did you go to movies or concerts? Did you eat out?

To heal your marriage you must rebuild your romance. Be intentional about going back and doing the things that once drew you close together. Be creative in re-building those experiences. Fully engage with them. Focus on recapturing each other's heart.

Why? Because marriage researchers have found that couples who re-create and re-engage in former romantic practices eventually fall back into their earlier feelings of love, romance, and enjoyment together. The intensity of your desire for each other might actually deepen. Your intimacy could be exponentially stronger than before the affair began.

Intimacy and romance usher in healing and protection of your marriage. We strongly urge you to re-engage in making love once you both commit to rebuilding your marriage. It is essential to create new sexual memories together. Lovemaking is a symbol of your oneness before God and your renewed commitment to your covenant. It strengthens your unity and shields you from spiritual attacks. (Your counselor will help you walk through the triggers this may create especially for the offended.)

Be attentive to the little things that each of you does to connect. Respond to your spouse. Show appreciation. One of the things Brad did was write Heidi love notes on a regular basis. This helped him retrain his mind as he looked for positive things about Heidi. It created a deeper appreciation and respect for her as his wife and friend.

Heidi would buy Brad something at the grocery store that he would enjoy eating. She also purchased little gifts as surprises for him. The things you do toward each other that are romantic and loving don't have to be huge, but they need to be evident and intentional.

BE SUPPORTIVE

No one will be as intimately involved with your recovery process as your spouse. You'll have conversations no one else will hear. You'll feel emotions no one else will know. You'll have reactions no one else will observe. You'll have days of discouragement and days of elation shared only by the two of you.

So pay attention to how you support one another. Even though you are walking different journeys of healing, you are called upon to encourage and build each other up. You are on the same team.

For example, it is not uncommon for the offended to feel like they "weren't enough." If you're the offender, you need to bring your spouse lots of reassurance. Yes, you strayed, and that makes it more challenging to come across as authentic. But over time your efforts will reaffirm your spouse. Tell your spouse how attractive they are to you. Tell them what you admire about their character and personality. Communicate to your spouse that the reasons for straying were character issues within you. It wasn't because they "weren't enough" for you.

In a similar way, as the offender you carry waves of shame, guilt, and fear that you won't be fully accepted or received because of what you did. When those waves come, you'll need to lean on your own personal strength and relationship with God. You must acknowledge truth, even if it may not resonate with your feelings at the time.

As the offended, you have an important role in helping your spouse recover. You will have to tell them:

- The truth is that they are forgiven.
- The truth is they are no longer judged by God for their sin. Instead, Jesus already paid the price for the sin that was committed.
- The truth is that while there are consequences, you are going to face them together.
- The truth is you still love them. You are committed to them and choose them.

- The truth is shame is not from God and ongoing guilt is not from God. That is an attack from the enemy.

There may be days when you *both* feel discouraged. Then you'll have to remind each other that God is big enough. Or something might trigger an emotional response. You simply need to be gracious and understand that those triggers are a consequence of the sin that was committed. Give grace in the midst of volatile and rolling emotions. It's vital as you progress.

EXPECT SPIRITUAL WARFARE

When you made the decision to stay together, all of heaven rejoiced! God is all about healing, reconciliation, and restoration. From cover to cover the Bible describes God's activity in making that happen. Just look at the cross! That's the most prominent example of what God did to restore our broken relationship with him.

At the same time, when you committed to stay together, hell mustered its forces against the two of you. Jesus described the enemy's ultimate goal when he said, "The thief comes only to steal and kill and destroy" (John 10:10). You've already experienced that attack through his efforts to kill your marriage, steal your joy, and destroy your witness. So expect a very specific, continuing barrage against the two of you, from the unseen spiritual realm.

The apostle Peter writes, "Your adversary the devil prowls around like a roaring lion, seeking someone to devour" (1 Peter 5:8). Be on your guard against him!

You may see each other as the enemy. And certainly, that is one of his tactics. Satan wants to minimize your awareness of the darkness attacking you. He wants you to attribute your troubles to each other instead of himself.

This topic of spiritual warfare may be new to you, but you must become familiar with it. As you begin on a new path of recovery with Jesus at the center of your relationship, you'll have to establish new practices for the protection of your marriage. You must unite in your stance against these attacks. So how do you do this?

When you start to have dark thoughts toward each other, recognize that the enemy whispers those thoughts to your mind. He plants thoughts like:

1. "It's hopeless. Your spouse is never going to change. You might as well give up and move on!"

2. "There they go again. It's the same old thing all over again. What's the use?"

3. "Maybe you should have never left that other relationship. You were happier the way things were. This is too hard!"

4. "They are asking too much of you. You shouldn't have to keep putting up with this!"

When this happens, take the thought captive and immediately replace it with what is true. So, for each of the examples above you might replace it with:

1. "That thought is not true. Nothing is hopeless where God is at work! Change is incremental. We might take two steps forward and one step back, but we are making progress! God has called me to persevere and stay committed."

2. "I'm going to give grace in this situation. I know they are well-intended and want to change. Perhaps God is allowing this to develop something stronger in me."

3. "God has called me to be a person of integrity and commitment. He will honor my efforts to do what is right. That other relationship was sin, and not true to who I am or to my commitment to Jesus. I did the right thing to leave and break it off."

4. "The things that are being asked of me are for the betterment of our marriage and the development of my character. God has not called me to only do easy

things. He has also called me to do hard things for his glory."

When you identify a spiritual attack from the enemy, make a verbal declaration, out loud, commanding him to leave. Because of your faith in Jesus Christ, you are able to speak with Jesus' authority. And so, with every spiritual attack that you identify, in your own words declare something like,

"In the name, power, and authority of the resurrected Jesus Christ who shed his blood for me, I command you to leave and go where Jesus sends you. You have no authority over me, my mind, or my marriage!"

REJECT THE "HERO" VS. "HEEL" MENTALITY

Sometimes when we speak at a conference or event, we tell part of our story. It's always sobering to see couples react to the pain that we experienced. One aspect of sharing our past that I (Heidi) struggle with is the mistaken perception that I'm a hero and Brad isn't. Honestly, I think it takes a lot more courage and humility to talk about your sin and poor choices publicly than it does to forgive a repentant spouse. To me, the real hero in our marriage is Brad.

Once you determine to rebuild your marriage, you too will encounter judgmental attitudes and reactions from others. Even if you don't talk about the infidelity, friends and family members will still reach their own conclusions. People may subconsciously classify the offended as the "hero" and the offender as the "heel."

Just remember the two of you are unified; you're on the same team. It's not beneficial or Christ-honoring to fault-find when you're trying to rebuild your marriage. When one of you is blessed by the Lord, the other one shares those same benefits and blessings. When Brad gets a raise, promotion, or special recognition, Heidi is a recipient as well of the good that comes from that. This is a time for unity. Cheer each other on because you are both heroes for rebuilding your marriage.

So don't refer to one spouse as "the good one" and the other as "the one who messed up." Don't take sarcastic jabs at the offender, or remind them of their past sin to shame them, or to use it against them. Once your spouse confesses and receives God's forgiveness and yours, move on from all that. The Bible tells us in Isaiah 43:25 that God "will not remember your sins." If the Lord doesn't remember your spouse's sins, why should you use their sins against them?

Heidi didn't desire to shame Brad, but she did need context around what happened. She had questions and she wanted answers. Eventually, she developed a filter as a check on her mind. Before you mention your spouse's affair ask these questions:

1. Am I bringing this up to shame or blame?

2. Do I want to discuss this so my spouse can be reminded of how they hurt me or our family?

3. Am I feeling insecure or sad today?

4. Is there any degree of pride, accusation, or self-vindication present in me?

If the answer to any of those questions is "yes", then don't bring up their infidelity. If the answer is "no", then continue to evaluate your own motives by asking:

5. Am I referencing the affair to understand my spouse better?

6. Will mentioning the sin help us avoid a destructive pattern of communication or conflict?

7. Will my words build greater intimacy and trust between us?

8. What's my motive for raising this issue?

Ultimately, only you and the Lord know your motives. But if your motives are right and you truly desire to strengthen your marriage, then bring up the issue, but only on rare occasions. As you and your spouse heal, you should reference the infidelity less often. Concentrate instead on the progress you've made in rebuilding your marriage.

PRAY TOGETHER

Your marriage was devastated by infidelity, yet you are on the road to recovery. As a couple you have been impacted relationally, spiritually, and emotionally. Rebuilding your marriage must take place from the inside out, through the work of God's Spirit. When you pray together you open your hearts to God's plan for your marriage.

We know this is probably new for you. In fact, over 90 percent of couples say they don't pray together every day. You need to be the exception, not the rule. Couples tell us this is the single most important thing they do to strengthen their marriage, other than becoming a follower of Jesus Christ.

Here are some ideas of what you can pray for:

- Pray for one another's healing.
- Pray that forgiveness would permeate your marriage.
- Pray for each other's growth in relationship with Jesus.
- Pray for your thoughts, words, and actions (mind, mouth, and motion) to be Christ-like.
- Pray that your spouse will stand strong under attack.
- Pray for protection.
- Pray for your spouse's growth in their relationship with Jesus Christ.

- Pray that they will desire to honor Jesus no matter what.

- Ask God to pour out his blessings and his favor upon you as you seek to honor him with your restoration.

Your times of prayer shouldn't be totally centered on rebuilding your marriage. Pray about people or situations that matter to you both. Pray about work and your finances. Pray for your children and friends, too.

Your prayers don't have to be anything long or flowery. Just begin with a simple prayer. Pray something like:

"Dear God,

Our marriage is in trouble and hurting. We don't know what to do but we need your help. Please guide us and draw us together. Heal our marriage and change us. Strengthen us. Grow our commitment to each other and you. Help us forgive where we need to.

In Jesus' name. Amen."

REMEMBER: GOD IS BIG ENOUGH

You've decided to rebuild your marriage. That's huge! You've decided to address broken places in your relationship. You're choosing to face imperfections in your character. You've committed to hard work in making things right. You're praying together. All of this will take time, effort, grace, mercy, perseverance and sheer will.

There will be times of discouragement. Count on it. You will have days when it seems like nothing is happening. Sometimes you will feel like it's hopeless. But it's not! You are moving from ruined to recovery.

You can have confidence in your process because God is in the middle of it all. This assurance does not ultimately rest in you and your spouse. Your confidence is in the One who brings his almighty power to bear in your restorative efforts.

Think about some of the accounts in the Bible of what God has done. He created the heavens, the earth, and everything in them. He took care of over 2 million people, the people of Israel, when they left Egypt. They wandered in a desert for 40 years and God brought food six days a week to feed them. Even their clothes and sandals didn't wear out while they were in the desert!

God took care of Noah and his family during the flood. David found his strength in the Lord when he went head-to-head against a giant and warrior named Goliath, and in God's power brought him down. God protected Daniel when he was thrown into the lion's den. He came out unscathed.

God healed withered limbs, made the blind to see, the mute to speak, and the deaf to hear! God raised the dead. He conquered death by raising Jesus from the grave.

And the same God who did all of this *is big enough* to heal and restore your marriage. Don't give up hope. Don't give up faith. Your confidence is in God. He is your strength, your firm foundation, your hope and your healer!

CELEBRATE THE WINS

Your marriage has been rocked to the core. You know that. That's why it is so critical to look for the victories in your journey, however small they may be. Let's say you're facing a tough decision. You work it out respectfully and in unity. That's a win!

Maybe you delve back into the discussion of what happened during the affair. Or you assess issues in your relationship prior to the affair. This time, however, you do it without blame or shame. You've just reached a milestone! When you have a difficult conversation that ends well and is still gut-wrenchingly honest, you are successful. Recognize and celebrate that!

The offended might get to the place where they can go a day or even a week without thinking about the betrayal. That may seem impossible right now, but Heidi is sometimes able to go a month or longer without it even crossing her mind. Any loosening of the chains of that memory is something to celebrate.

As you rebuild your marriage, recognize milestones. For us, one of the biggest days of the year is our anniversary. It's like a national holiday. Our anniversary is a day we commemorate what God is doing in each of us and in our marriage. Once we were on the brink of imploding. Now, by the grace of God, we are more happily married than we have *ever* been.

Likewise, you make deposits into your life and marriage when you honor each other. Celebrate and take a special trip to a romantic destination. Invite friends over for a party to remember God's goodness to you. Spend the day together or renew your wedding vows. These mini-celebrations unify you and recalibrate your focus on the good things happening in your marriage.

TURN YOUR PAIN TO PURPOSE

One of our favorite Bible verses comes from the apostle Paul's letter to the church in Rome. He writes, "And we know that for those who love God all things work together for good, for those who are called according to his purpose" (Romans 8:28). God is the one who takes even the most painful, horrible betrayal and turns it around for his glory.

If you need an example, all you have to do is look at what happened when Jesus was betrayed. Judas betrayed him. The disciples abandoned him. The crowds shouted, "Crucify him!" He suffered an unjust death for you and me. But God took that injustice, he used that betrayal and he turned it around for the greatest glory.

Every one of us who places our faith and trust in Jesus Christ experiences not only the forgiveness of sins, but eternal life now and forever. We enjoy the intimacy of a relationship with our heavenly Father. We live with the empowerment of the Holy Spirit in our lives. God brings good out of what was evil.

In our journey we have found 2 Corinthians 1:3-4 gives us good direction for how to handle the mess we experienced. It says, "Blessed be the God and Father of our Lord Jesus Christ, the Father of mercies and God of all comfort, who comforts us in all our affliction, so that we may be able to comfort those who are in any affliction, with the comfort with which we ourselves are comforted by God."

As we receive peace and healing we are able to comfort others who are in similar situations. God's mercy is always greater than our mistakes. He takes our messes and turns them into ministry!

For us, God called us to start Build Your Marriage a number of years ago. This ministry began as we moved from ruined to recovery. We weren't led to start a ministry centered around adultery and restoration, though. Marriage is so much bigger than that. Marital issues can be much more complex. So our driving desire in Build Your Marriage is to "*Help couples build a Christ-centered marriage.*"

Through the years we've had the opportunity to minister to countless couples around the world who are in the same situation you are in right now. We can give them the comfort that we ourselves have received from the Holy Spirit.

You may not speak to large audiences, your small group, or even your Sunday school class about your journey from ruined to recovery. That's fine. But you may come across another couple who is deeply wounded, hurt, and not sure where to turn. They need the help and counsel of someone that has seen God's hand at work in their lives in a similar situation.

Both of you will have split-second opportunities to share your story. Decide ahead of time that you will let God use you to bring the hope and comfort you received.

Don't worry about what you will say. Just be in agreement that, should the opportunity arise, you will come alongside the hurting person and provide the encouragement and direction they need. God will give you the words to say. In fact, the greatest testimony to a couple in crisis is a visual example of a couple reconciled, healed, and restored!

May God richly bless you as you continue on your journey of healing, recovery, and restoration. May he pour his Spirit upon you. The Spirit of peace, comfort, power, and truth will guide you all the days of your life as you submit to Jesus Christ and build a Christ-centered marriage to his glory!

ACKNOWLEDGMENTS

When our lives were ruined, God knew we needed a strong support system around us to help our marriage recover. Without the love and prayers of these individuals we don't think we'd be where we are today.

To our family, who were thrust into an immensely painful season of life and walked it with grace and love, we are so thankful for your encouragement and strength.

To Bob Barrows, our counselor, who gave us wise and sound counsel when we were so broken we couldn't think straight.

To Billy and Sharlie Twiddy, who selflessly opened your home and provided a safe place of healing and love.

To Woody and Robin Frey, Rob and Beth Hirschi, and the two men who flew to us in the first days of our crisis (you know who you are), thank you for being the hands and feet of Jesus in dark days and tangibly loving us.

To Dan and Kay Fekete and Randy and Kathy Wright, who infused hope with your physical presence on a regular basis.

To our dear friends, Dave and Teresa Anderson, Melanie Dart, Darrin Dodge, Dave Howland, Mark and Heidi Mittelberg, Lee and Leslie Strobel, Steve and Sallie Whelan,

Steve and Luann Willemin, and Ron and Natalie Willmarth, your friendship brought a smile to our hearts and buoyed our spirits time and again when we needed it the most. Thanks for your faithful prayers.

To our couples small group from Michigan, you circled the wagons around us and made us feel safe in a turbulent time.

To Dr. Jim Austin and Rev. Rick Astle, your conversations with Brad gave him hope for the future in some form of ministry.

To the elders, staff, and congregation at The River Church, we are forever grateful for your ongoing support and belief in our ministry to couples through Build Your Marriage. We love serving Jesus with you.

To Tom and Sara Gilson, for your steady friendship. Tom, we are grateful for your wisdom and editorial insights.

To the countless others who reached out to us when we just didn't have the energy to respond, your words and prayers mean more to us than you will ever know.

Build Your Marriage® is a non-profit ministry with a mission *to help couples build a Christ-centered marriage.* Through marriage conferences, events, retreats, published resources, blogs and social media, the ministry resources and strengthens couples around the world. You can learn more about Build Your Marriage® and their resources at BuildYourMarriage.org.

Connect with us!

 BuildYourMarriage.org

 Facebook.com/BuildYourMarriage

 @BuildUrMarriage

 BuildYourMarriage

Additional Resources

Also from Build Your Marriage® and available on Amazon:

Take your marriage deeper by connecting every day with your spouse! This book contains 366 questions covering a variety of topics. Each discussion is designed to stimulate connection. Every page has space for each spouse to record their responses as a future keepsake as well.

Learn about couples of the Bible and the real-life issues they faced in this nine-session small group study. Available for download or purchase wherever books are sold.